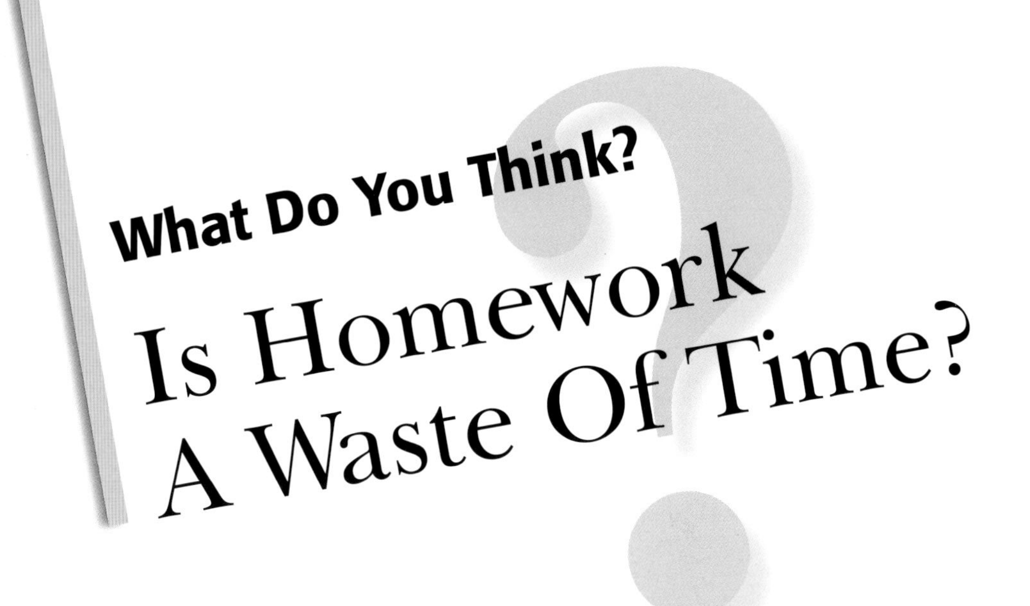

Kate Shuster

www.heinemann.co.uk/library
Visit our website to find out more information about Heinemann Library books.

To order:
Phone 44 (0) 1865 888112
Send a fax to 44 (0) 1865 314091
Visit the Heinemann bookshop at www.heinemann.co.uk/library to browse our catalogue and order online.

First published in Great Britain by Heinemann Library, Halley Court, Jordan Hill, Oxford OX2 8EJ, part of Harcourt Education.

Heinemann is a registered trademark of Harcourt Education Ltd.

Editorial: Andrew Farrow and Rebecca Vickers
Design: Steve Mead and Q2A Solutions
Picture Research: Melissa Allison
Production: Alison Parsons

Originated by Chroma Graphics Pte. Ltd.
Printed and bound in China by Leo Paper Group

ISBN 978 0 431 11013 4

12 11 10 09 08
10 9 8 7 6 5 4 3 2 1

British Library Cataloguing in Publication Data
Shuster, Kate, 1974-
Is homework a waste of time? – (What do you think?)
1.Homework – Juvenile literature
I. Title
371.3'0281

ISBN-13: 9780431110134

Acknowledgements
The publishers would like to thank the following for permission to reproduce photographs:

©Alamy p. **4** (Photofusion Picture Library); ©Corbis pp. **44**, **41** top right,bottom right, bottom left, **42** (Andrew Brookes), **6** (Ariel Skelley), **10**, **12**, **50** (Brand X/Rob Melnychuk), **48** (Rob Lewine); ©Getty Images pp. **8** (Alex and Laila), **41** top left (PhotoDisc); ©Harcourt Education Ltd p. **35** (Tudor Photography); ©istockphoto pp. **32**, **38** (Alberto Pomares), **16** (Kurt Gordon), **36** (Nancy Louie); ©PhotoEdit, Inc. p. **24** (David Young-Wolff), **7** (Michael Newman), **39** (Tony Freeman); ©Photolibrary p. **46** (Photononstop); ©Punchstock p. **20** (Blend Images); ©Randy Glasbergen p. **30**; ©Reportdigital.co.uk p. **43** (Paul Box); ©Science Photo Library pp. **28** (Hank Morgan), **14** (RIA Novosti), p. **18** Courtesy of Alfie Kohn.

Cover photograph reproduced with permission of TIPS/Blend Images. Blackboard frame from ©Blackboard.

Every effort has been made to contact copyright holders of any material reproduced in this book. Any omissions will be rectified in subsequent printings if notice is given to the publishers.

The publishers would like to thank Lindsay Thorne for her assistance with the preparation of this book.

Table of Contents

Some words are shown in bold, **like this**. You can find out what they mean by looking in the glossary.

> *What do you think?*

All over the world, pupils are given homework every night. Sometimes there is so much homework that students don't have time to relax, play sport, or even get a full night's sleep. Is all this homework worth it? Or is homework a waste of time?

Is Homework A Waste Of Time?

This book is about homework. If you're like most children, you're given some homework every day. You probably already have opinions about homework. Perhaps you think that some homework helps you understand your schoolwork, while other homework is a waste of time. But are you right? Is there good evidence to support your opinion? Or is there better **evidence** for the opposite point of view?

The purpose of this book is to present evidence for both sides in the debate about homework. This will help you to develop your own informed opinion. You'll need to put aside your personal experiences and beliefs and consider both sides with an open mind. Having an open mind means that you are willing to learn about different perspectives on an issue. Then you can make a decision about which one is most likely to be true. In this book, you'll read the opinions of experts, teachers, pupils, and parents about homework. You'll learn about how researchers study the effects of homework, including its pros and cons. And by the time you finish the book (which you may be reading as homework!), you'll be able to answer the question under examination: "Is homework a waste of time?"

Thinking critically

The purpose of this book is to help you develop the skills of **critical thinking**. Critical thinking involves careful consideration of many perspectives on an issue. Critical thinkers don't jump to conclusions about issues or assume that their opinion is the correct one. Instead, they look at the available evidence and then decide which opinion they think is the best one.

> *How much is too much?*

Young people spend most of their day at school. Is it fair or necessary to ask pupils to spend time after school working on school projects and homework?

This is especially hard when considering an issue such as homework. You have lots of experience and opinions about it, and it's hard to set aside your own perspective to give other ideas a fair hearing. But ideas that don't agree with your experience often turn out to be correct. Sometimes these ideas are **counterintuitive**–they go against your expectations about an issue. For example, humans once believed the Earth was flat, based on their own observations. But over time, scientific observation showed the Earth was actually round. Human intuition was wrong.

Sometimes even ideas that are well thought out can be wrong. For example, many people avoided travelling on planes after the terrorist attacks of 11 September 2001. They believed that air travel had become more dangerous. Instead, people chose to drive, because they thought cars would be safer than planes. But this expectation turned out to be wrong. Car travel is more dangerous than air travel, even including the risk of a terrorist attack. Studies by leading economists have shown that with more people on the roads, there were four times more fatal car accidents in the United States after the 9/11 attacks.

> *Skill building*

Teachers who set homework don't do it to torture pupils. They do it to help them understand their lessons and improve their skills in subjects such as maths and science.

It is natural to believe that your views are the correct ones, especially when dealing with issues that are important to you. But critical thinkers try to set aside their own opinions so that they can give issues fair consideration. **Bias** is generally the opposite of fairness. We say that people are biased when their viewpoints prevent them from considering opposing ideas. The lesson here is that sometimes your opinions are just opinions. Until they're supported by reasons and evidence, they're not sufficiently informed.

Reasons and evidence

As you form your opinions about homework and other issues, it's important to make sure that these opinions are supported. When you express your opinion as an **argument** in favour of a particular point of view, you need to include **reasoning** and evidence to back up your position.

Reasoning is the "because" part of an argument. It shows why your position is more likely to be true than false. Let's say you believe that television is a bad influence. By itself, that statement doesn't have any support. Adding reasoning will make it more persuasive:

- Television is a bad influence, because people spend time watching television instead of doing useful activities.

> *The importance of critical thinking*
>
> **Research and critical thinking skills can help you succeed in any school subject, because all school subjects require problem-solving skills and the ability to read carefully and draw your own conclusions.**

The "because" statement offers support for your initial idea. But reasoning isn't enough—you also need evidence for your arguments. Evidence is fact, example, or other support for your reasoning. Here are three ways of adding evidence to the example above:

- Television is a bad influence, because people spend time watching television instead of doing useful activities. For example, the average person spends three hours a day watching television. If they exercised for half that time, they'd burn hundreds of calories.
- Television is a bad influence, because people spend time watching television instead of doing useful activities. For example, people who watch a lot of television don't read as many books. But reading books helps us improve our memory and vocabulary, unlike television.
- Television is a bad influence, because people spend time watching television instead of doing useful activities. According to a study by the Kaiser Family Foundation, children who watch a lot of TV are less likely to spend time doing things with their parents.

Whether you express your arguments in a speech, in conversation with friends, or in a written essay, including reasoning and evidence will always make your opinions more powerful and harder to knock down.

Evidence

Evidence comes in many different forms. Just as a house's foundations make it strong, evidence supports your reasoning and ideas and keeps your arguments from falling down. As you consider the facts, you will also have to make sure you are getting information from qualified and reliable sources. Here are several kinds of evidence you might encounter:

Examples. The most basic kind of evidence. These can be personal examples, historical examples, or hypothetical (imaginary) examples.

Studies. Results of scientific and academic examination of a topic. There are many kinds of study, and some are better than others. It's important to understand studies well before using them to support your position.

Statistics. Numbers representing descriptions of events. Statistics are usually generated by studies, so the cautions about studies apply to statistics, too.

Expert testimony. Quotes from experts can show support for your position.

> *Homework—a recent development*

Homework is part of the school experience for most pupils today. Even very young pupils may be given homework, with the amounts increasing as they get older. But this wasn't always true. In fact, homework has only been an important part of most pupils' lives in the last 70 years.

History Of Homework

Although most pupils today take homework for granted as a basic part of going to school, homework hasn't always been a significant part of schooling. A hundred years ago, teachers and parents were extremely critical of homework. Many doctors, too, argued that homework injured children's spines and damaged their minds and nerves. In 1901, the state of California passed a law banning homework for children up to year 10, and limiting homework for older children.

Now, however, most children do homework as part of going to school—a lot of homework. In Japan, 14-year-olds do an average of eight and a half hours every week. In other countries such as Italy, Poland, and Israel, teenagers do eight or nine hours a week. Children in Britain, the United States, and Australia do less, but they still average six hours a week.

This is a lot of homework. But to put these numbers into perspective, consider that children in Britain, the United States, and Australia also spend more than 20 hours a week watching television. Between television, homework, meals, sleep, and school, it's amazing that children have any time at all for other pursuits such as sport, dance, music, or art.

"A waste of time and energy"

At the beginning of the twentieth century, many people began to protest at what they saw as too much homework being given to children in schools. They called for educational reform, arguing that "home study" caused mental and physical fatigue in children. Homework was widely believed to be "unnatural" and dangerous. In 1900, a famous anti-homework article called "A National Crime at the Feet of American Parents" appeared in the *Ladies' Home Journal*, one of the most widely read magazines in the United States at the turn of the century. Those who opposed homework thought that home study interfered with children's ability to just be children, instead training them to be like adults.

The basis for these ideas was something called the child study movement. Its founder, psychologist G. Stanley Hall, believed that all humans move through distinct stages of growth that are determined by biology. He argued that rushing children to adulthood through excessive schoolwork would interfere with their movement through these stages and severely damage their mental and physical health. Hall and his followers were against children going to school before the age of eight. His ideas were very popular in the United States and elsewhere, and encouraged many schools (especially in the United States) to ban homework altogether.

> *G. Stanley Hall (1844–1924)*

Hall's pioneering work in childhood development was influential all over the world. He is considered the "father" of American psychology.

Homework and health

Popular criticism of homework continued until after the Second World War (1939–1945). Some doctors warned that homework would damage children's eyes (from overuse) and permanently damage their spines (from carrying heavy books). Homework might cause lost sleep, tuberculosis, heart disease, "nerve shock", and even death.

Critics argued that homework deprived children of chances to play, exercise, practise music, help around the house, and spend time with their parents and family. One school official called it "a waste of time and energy". Schools were supposed to nurture children's interests instead of imposing rigid rules and behaviour on them.

150 years ago

Homework wasn't always an important part of going to school. Here are some other things that are different about school now compared to 150 years ago:

Universal attendance. Today, school is compulsory for all children, and there are penalties for not attending. Education became compulsory at about the same time that the industrialized world ended widespread child labour. Most people agreed that it was better for children to go to school than to work in factories.

Inclusive education. In most of the developed world, education now is for everyone, not just the wealthy, white, and male. But 150 years ago, education was a privilege available to a select few.

Different subjects. Most people going to school 150 years ago learned mainly basic maths and reading. If pupils studied another language, it was almost always Latin or Greek.

Calendar. Because children of farmers had to help with spring planting and autumn harvests, most schools were open only in the winter and summer. Farming parents couldn't afford to let their children spend time doing homework when there were chores to do around the farm.

Mixed years. Most schools had only one or two teachers. Children of all ages would be in a single class together, not separated into year groups. In some schools boys and girls were taught separately.

"A Nation at Risk"

In 1957, opinions about homework changed dramatically in the Western world. The Soviet Union's launch of the Sputnik spacecraft caused quite a panic in many Western nations. At the height of the Cold War, it seemed that the Soviets were winning the space race, and other countries were desperate to compete effectively with their advancements. Suddenly, education magazines and politicians everywhere were calling for more rigorous educational methods, including homework. The idea was that to have more and better scientists, we would need more and better schools.

> *Competition and progress*

In many countries, educational achievement is associated with scientific progress and a push for national advancement. In the United States, there was a renewed emphasis on homework and rigid educational standards after the Soviet Union launched its Sputnik spacecraft (shown above), the world's first artificial satellite.

The final boost for homework came in 1983, when the administration of U.S. President Ronald Reagan issued a report called *A Nation At Risk*. This report argued that nations without extremely rigorous educational systems were losing out to countries such as Japan and Korea, where education was emphasized more strongly. "The educational foundations of our society are presently being eroded by a rising tide of **mediocrity** that threatens our very future as a nation and a people," said the report. Its message influenced education from the United States to Australia. For decades, homework had been the enemy, but now it was ready for a comeback.

An overreaction?

Educational researchers Brian Gill and Steven Schlossman argue that the release of this report made schools give pupils more and more homework, even very young children. "Before the 1980s," says Gill, "it didn't really occur to anyone to assign homework to kids who were young enough that they weren't reading."

Meeting new standards

The change to what is called **standards-based education** spread to Europe and Australia. This may seem like an insignificant development, since most education was already based on standards. For example, even hundreds of years ago, schools had basic requirements for pupils, such as memorizing multiplication tables, following rules of grammar, and reciting poetry. But in modern practice, standards-based education demands that teachers and students meet standards that are set and enforced by governments. It also makes education more standardized, so that all children of the same age get the same basic education.

How did homework fit into this new craze for standards and standardization? The idea was that if children did more homework and worked hard on schoolwork outside school, they would be more likely to improve in their lessons and achieve the standards set. The push for more challenging educational systems meant that everyone, including pupils, would play a part in making sure that performance was high and standards were being met. So the arguments about homework damaging children's bodies and minds were dismissed, and the new age of homework began.

> *What's your view?*

School can be lots of fun, with opportunities to learn about all kinds of things, from what makes plants grow to the history of the world. But school can also be a chore, with homework that is difficult and takes up a lot of time. Is all that homework really valuable, or is it a waste of time?

Homework Points of View

You've read a little bit about past debates on the value of homework. Now it's time to see what some experts have to say. In this chapter, you'll read two opposing points of view on homework. The first article, by author Alfie Kohn, makes the argument that homework is bad. The writer claims that pupils get too much homework. The second article, by researchers Brian Gill and Steven Schlossman, argues that pupils don't get too much homework. They believe that homework can be very valuable.

Each article is from a major newspaper, with the authors making an argument about the value of homework. Both articles present evidence, using research, **statistics**, studies, and quotations to support their points. Consider the evidence carefully, and make up your own mind about what you've read.

The articles contain some vocabulary words that you might not know. Some of these words are briefly explained within the text. You can also look up words in the glossary at the back of this book, or in a dictionary. But overall, you should be able to understand the major arguments in the articles and be able to explain the evidence that supports each point of view.

> *Alfie Kohn*

Article author Alfie Kohn is a writer and lecturer on education, human behaviour, and parenting.

Kids May Be Right After All: Homework Stinks
By Alfie Kohn

With the start of the new school year, students once again are shifting impatiently in their seats, working their way through an endless pile of worksheets. And that's after they come home.

A new study confirms what kids and parents already know: The "tougher standards" fad that has American education in its grip has meant more and more homework for younger and younger children.

Several years ago, we learned that the proportion of 6- to 8-year-olds who reported having homework on a given day had climbed from 34% in 1981 to 58% in 1997 and that the weekly time spent studying more than doubled during the same period.

Last month, professor Sandra Hofferth at the University of Maryland released an update to that study. Now, the proportion of young children who had homework on a specific day jumped to 64%, and the time they spent on it climbed by another third. Homework rates for 6- to 8-year-olds are virtually equivalent to those for 9- to 12-year-olds. And let's not talk about the high school workload.

What the research shows is disconcerting. Equally important, however, is what the research doesn't show: that homework is necessary or beneficial.We know all about the stress and exhaustion, the family conflict and loss of time from other activities. ("Our kids are missing out on their childhoods," one Mom laments.) But we reassure ourselves that it's all worth it because homework raises achievement, teaches independence and good work habits and helps them become successful learners. Remarkably, however, the data to support those beliefs just don't exist:

- There is no evidence that homework provides any benefits in elementary school. Even if you regard standardized test results as a useful measure (which I don't), homework isn't even *associated* with higher scores at this age. The only effect that does show up is more negative attitudes on the part of students who got more assignments.
- In high school, some studies do find a **correlation** between homework and test scores (or grades), but it's usually fairly small and it has a tendency to disappear when more sophisticated statistical controls are applied. Moreover, there's no evidence that higher achievement is down to the homework even when an association does appear.
- International comparisons offer no reassurance. In describing the results of their analysis of student performance across 50 countries, which was published last year, Pennsylvania State University researchers David Baker and Gerald LeTendre said: "Not only did we fail to find any positive relationships," but "the overall correlations between national average student achievement and national averages (in amount of homework assigned)… are all negative."
- Finally, not a single study has ever supported the claim that homework teaches good work habits or develops positive character traits such as self-discipline and independence. These assumptions could be described as urban myths except for the fact that they're still taken seriously in suburban and rural areas, too.

In short, the research provides no reason to think students would be at any sort of disadvantage if they got less homework—or maybe none at all. And the accounts I've heard from teachers and schools that have abolished after-school assignments, yet whose students are succeeding brilliantly (while maintaining their enthusiasm about learning), offer evidence of a different sort.

Yet these schools are in the minority. As a rule, homework is assigned not merely on those occasions when the teacher believes it might help, but on a regular schedule that's been determined ahead of time. And the homework load is growing fastest for younger children, which is where the supporting evidence isn't just shaky—it's non-existent.

It's time for us to stop taking the value of homework for granted. Rather than confining ourselves to peripheral questions—"What types of binders should kids have?" "Is X minutes enough time for this assignment?"—we should ask what really matters: Is the kind of homework our kids are getting worth doing in any amount? What evidence exists to show that daily homework is necessary for children to become better thinkers or more engaged learners?

(continued on page 20)

And: What if, after spending six or seven hours a day at school, we let them have their afternoons and evenings just to be kids?
[From *USA Today*, 14 September 2006, p.13A
http://www.usatoday.com/printedition/news/20060914/a_opcom14.art.htm]

> *Are pupils overloaded?*

Many people think pupils have too much homework, and that their workload is increasing. Others have the opposite opinion. These form the two sides in the 'homework war'.

My Dog Ate My Argument: *The claim that kids get too much homework just doesn't stand up*
By Brian P. Gill and Steven L. Schlossman

At the turn of the century, Edward Bok, the powerful editor of the *Ladies' Home Journal*, launched an impassioned campaign against homework, arguing that it crippled the physical, mental, and emotional health of children. He branded it "a national crime at the feet of American parents." The U.S. commissioner of education agreed, telling Congress that homework was "a prolific source of abuse." A year later, in 1901, California—along with dozens of local school districts across the country—banned homework altogether for any public school child under 15.

Today, concern about homework is again reaching a fever pitch. The most recent round is prompted by reports since the mid-1990s that the homework load is higher than ever. The *New York Times*, for instance, reported that children are "homework-bound" by the "gross tonnage" of homework. *USA Today* reported that the nation was in a period of "homework intensification".

These homework wars are a familiar part of the nation's ongoing debate over education. Since Bok's day, the pendulum has swung back and forth. One generation of educators worries that students are not getting enough of it (this happened in the 1950s and 1980s). The next generation worries that children are overworked and overscheduled and that their social development is being ignored.

But today's war, like those that preceded it, is based on several false notions. The first is that there's a huge and growing homework burden. That perception is completely contrary to the evidence.

Two new studies—one by us and one by Tom Loveless of the Brookings Institution—make clear that the great majority of American children at all ages do only moderate amounts of homework. When asked, for instance, how much homework they did "yesterday", most children across the country—in elementary, middle and high school grades—said they do no more than an hour.

And this is not unique to our times. It turns out there was no "golden age" when most American kids, willingly or unwillingly, did lots of homework. Since World War II, the proportion of high school students spending a substantial amount of time studying—more than two hours nightly—has generally varied from 7% to 13%. Homework amounts peaked briefly during the decade after Sputnik but, even then, not more than one high school student in four studied more than two hours a night. Little homework is the norm and has always been the norm.

Second, it's not true that most parents object to homework. Today, as in the past, most parents strongly support it. A Public Agenda poll in 2000 found that only 10% of parents thought their children had too much homework, while 25% thought they had too little and 64% thought the amount was about right.

A vocal minority can often manage to get the media's attention—as Bok did, and as happened again in the 1930s, when homework was branded a "sin against childhood" by opponents. But it's just that: a noisy minority, not a representative sample of the population.

Third, and most important, the homework wars—this time as in the past—are narrowly centered on the quantity that is being assigned: How much is too much, and how much is too little? Very little effort goes into figuring out how to improve the quality and value of the homework that teachers assign.

In our view, homework is the prime window into the school for parents to see, understand, and connect with the academic mission of the teachers. It is the primary area in which children, parents and schools interact on a daily basis. Yet it gets less systematic thought and attention than any other key component of education. Other than the admonition [*an admonition is advice*] that kids should do more of it, we pay almost no attention to how to improve its design and content. Nor do we do much to prepare teachers to use and evaluate homework, to hold administrators accountable for monitoring the homework load, or to cultivate parents' collaboration. Homework remains an orphan child of the educational excellence movement.

The debate over homework must be redirected. Moral exhortation—accusing our kids and parents of being lazy, comparing them unfavorably with their counterparts in Japan (as in the 1980s) or Russia (as in the 1950s)—just doesn't seem to have much effect in changing long-term homework trends.

After half a century of failure to increase student buy-in, it's time to rethink how to make homework a more valued part of the pedagogic [*this means teaching*] process. In addition to promoting academic achievement, homework can inculcate [*inculcate means to develop or teach*] habits of self-discipline and independent study and can help inform parents about the educational agenda of their school. We must find ways to make homework an interesting and challenging educational experience for students, instead of the uniform, seat-bound, memorization-focused, solo exercise it has been. Otherwise, all our talk about high standards and improving student achievement will run up against the same roadblock that has stymied [*this means blocked or frustrated*] the pursuit of educational excellence in the past.

[This opinion article appeared in the *Los Angeles Times* on 11 December 2003. http://www.rand.org/commentary/121103LAT.html]

On the decline?

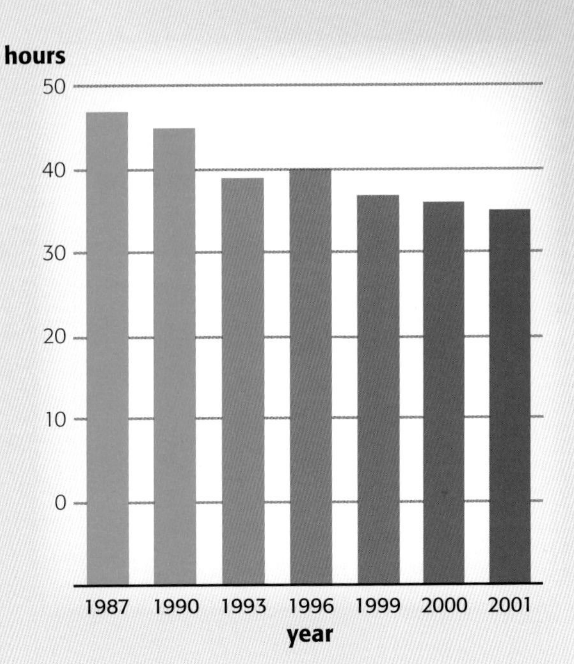

This graph, from the *Chronicle of Higher Education,* illustrates the amount of time spent studying at home by American sixth formers. The left axis represents the percentage of pupils who studied for six or more hours every week. The axis on the bottom marks the year pupils were surveyed, from 1987 to 2001. The results displayed here are similar to those mentioned by the authors of the *Los Angeles Times* article. By 2006, Dr Michael Kirst reported that 65% of incoming students at the University of California at Los Angeles did homework for five hours or less a week while in their last year at school.

What do you think?

The two articles disagree on a number of issues. Before deciding which article you found more persuasive, it's best to review the authors' major points.

The first article, "Kids May Be Right After All: Homework Stinks", criticizes homework. The author argues that children have too much homework, pointing to a new study that shows homework is increasing, especially for very young children. He also says that although most people think homework is good, studies do not show that it leads to success at school.

> *Homework's lasting influence*

Is homework helpful or harmful? The answer could affect educational milestones later in life, such as graduating from university.

Did you find these arguments persuasive? Why or why not? If the author is right about the evidence, what should we do about homework?

The humorous title of the second article, "My Dog Ate My Argument", refers to a common excuse pupils use to explain why they don't have their homework: that their dog ate it. The authors make three major points in the article. First, they say that the available evidence does not support the claim that pupils do too much homework. Second, they say that most parents do not object to the amount of homework given to children. Third, they argue that we need to concentrate more on making homework better and more useful, instead of worrying about how much is too much.

Did you find these arguments persuasive? Why or why not? What, according to the authors, are some of the benefits of homework?

Now compare the two articles. Which was more persuasive? Why? Did you notice that one article was from 2003 and one from 2006? Does this matter? Why or why not? Finally, both articles encourage us to focus on the kind of homework given. What do you think? Does the kind of homework matter? Are some assignments better than others?

What is a correlation?

In the "Homework Stinks" article, the author uses a concept called correlation that you may find unfamiliar. He writes: "In high school, some studies do find a correlation between homework and test scores (or grades)…." Saying that two things are correlated means that they are found together. They are co-related. For example, butter and cheese tend to be in the same place (a sandwich) at the same time (lunch), so they are correlated. Butter and cheese have a *positive correlation,* because where you find one thing, the other thing is likely to be there, too. What are some other things that have a positive correlation?

Later in the article, the author quotes a researcher talking about correlations being "negative". This means that when you find one thing, you are less likely to find the other thing. Chewing gum might be negatively correlated with crisps, because someone who is chewing gum is unlikely also to be eating crisps.

It is important to understand that just because two things are correlated, that doesn't necessarily mean that one thing causes the other thing. Butter may be found in the same place as cheese, but the presence of the butter did not cause the cheese to appear. All you can conclude is that the two things are often found together.

> *Does homework benefit students?*

Most children want to do well at school. Does homework help them with their schoolwork? Or does it have the opposite effect? There is quite a bit of debate about the relationship, if any, between homework and school success.

Thinking Critically About Homework

Pupils and their parents have been upset about homework for a very long time. As long ago as the 1880s, economist and educator Francis A. Walker, who was at the time the president of the Boston School Board, complained about his children's maths homework—"Over and over again have I had to send my own children... to bed, long after the assigned tasks had ceased to have any educational value and become a means of nervous exhaustion and agitation, highly prejudicial to body and mind."

Many pupils feel that they're asked to do too much work as part of going to school. Is all that work worth it? Why is homework supposed to be so good for children? And does it actually achieve the benefits that are claimed?

First, we examine some of the justifications for homework that have been offered by researchers, teachers, parents, and pupils. Do any of the arguments seem valid? Then we can explore how to study the effect of homework and use research to back up an argument.

What's homework for?

Most pupils spend between six and eight hours at school every day. Then they spend additional time doing homework. Homework varies according to teachers, subjects, and the year at school. Some homework is fairly basic, such as a set of maths problems. Other homework is more complex, such as researching a project or building a model. But what's all that homework for? In this section, we'll explore three of the major justifications for giving homework, and evaluate the reasoning and evidence for those claims. We'll also look at the arguments and evidence against these points.

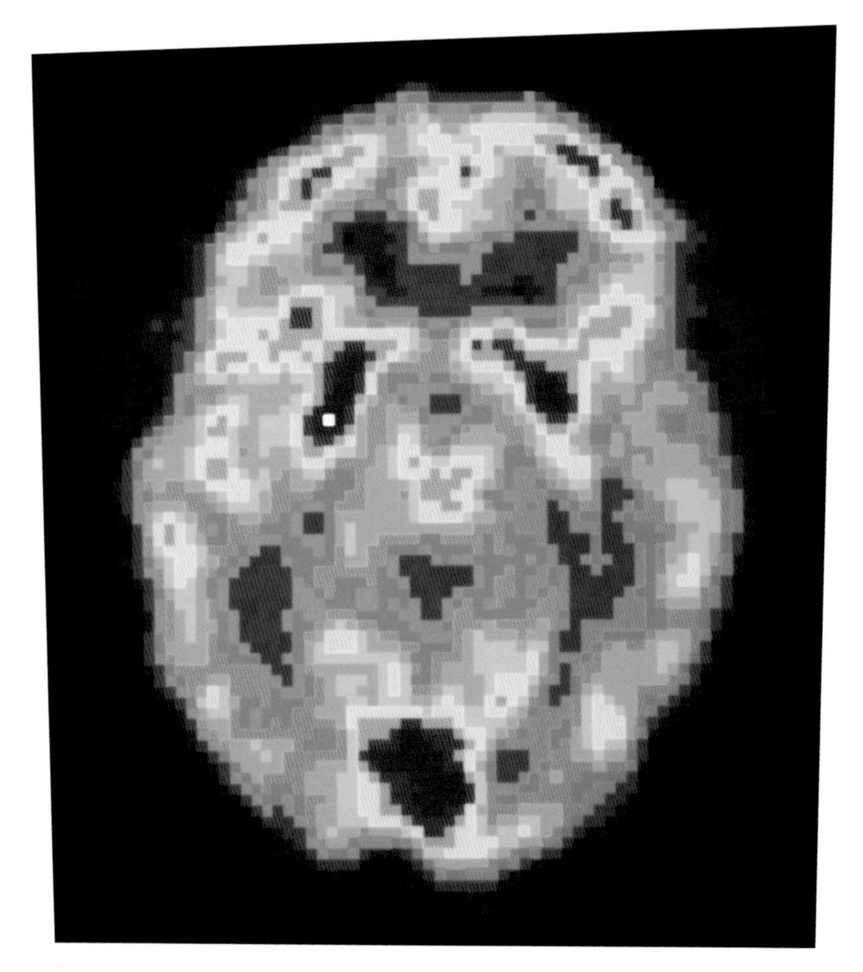

> *Watching the brain at work*

Understanding how the brain works can help us understand how we learn. Here, we see a brain "in action", using an imaging process that lets us see different parts of the awake brain at work. The red and yellow areas show more activity, while the blue and green areas show less activity.

The claim: Homework improves learning

The reasoning

At first, it would seem obvious that doing homework helps with learning. After all, if doing work at school helps you learn, then doing extra work at home should help you learn more or help you remember what you learned. The idea is that if you extend what education experts call the **time on task**, you will learn more. Ever hear that "practice makes perfect"? If you have, you've heard about time on task.

Your brain is made up of millions of tiny cells that form **cortical maps**. Those maps are made up of the pathways that connect different cells. Think about the ways in which roads connect houses, districts, and cities. As a city becomes busy and important, it builds a lot of roads that connect it to more and more places. On the other hand, if a city is mostly empty and no one ever visits it, fewer roads go there.

The brain works like this as well. It is "plastic", changing itself to support the different activities you do. This may help to explain how we learn. Repeatedly practising certain skills "rewires" the brain to support those skills. So the more we study, the more we should learn.

The evidence

In the 1980s, Dr Harris Cooper, at that time a professor of psychology at the University of Missouri-Columbia, analyzed a number of studies that compared children who received homework to children who did not. He found that "the average student doing homework in these studies had a higher achievement score than 55 percent of students not doing homework."

These effects seemed stronger for older pupils—in years 5, 6, and 7 the average pupil doing homework outscored about 52 percent of the pupils who were not doing homework. At secondary school up to year 10, the homework pupils did better than 60 percent of their peers. In years 11 to 13 they did better than 69 percent of the pupils who didn't do homework.

Other studies have shown that homework is positively related to good results. Professor Julian Betts of the University of California, San Diego, studied 6,000 children to see how their homework habits affected their school performance. He found that if they did an extra 30 minutes of maths homework every night, starting in year 8, they would achieve two grades above their expected level in year 12.

On the other hand...

Time on task may not be all that's relevant. In order to build new maps in our brains, we have to be paying attention to what we're doing. It requires too much energy for the brain to rewire itself every time we notice something or have a new experience. Researcher Anne Pycha explains that "it makes sense that the brain protects itself from random, whimsical change by requiring a real investment from us. Without our attention, without our willingness to practise intensively, the brain just won't budge. It already possesses too many valuable skills, either built-in or learned, to change without a good reason." So it's not just time on task that matters. You could spend a long time on a task, but if you're not paying attention, anything you learn is unlikely to "stick". This is why, if you've ever "crammed" by studying for an exam without truly caring about the information, you are likely to forget anything you learned.

What does this have to do with homework? It means that if children aren't engaged and interested in what they're learning, time spent on homework isn't necessarily going to help them understand the material. In fact, if the pupils find

> *Making excuses*

Many children find homework dull, but it does encourage them to become more creative in thinking up excuses to avoid doing it!

the material boring, they may be less likely to enjoy school-related tasks, rather than more likely. Boring homework may reduce their interest in school overall.

Also, the kind of learning involved in school homework may be very different from the kind of learning involved in playing a sport or a musical instrument. You can develop physical skills by practising a behaviour. But developing the skill of doing maths questions isn't necessarily the same as understanding maths. You could memorize all the relevant dates of French history but still not be able to explain why the French Revolution happened.

Finally, it's not necessarily the case that studies support the relationship between homework and academic achievement. The evidence is pretty mixed, as you've already seen from the extracts in the previous chapter. Author Alfie Kohn, in his book *The Homework Myth*, argues that most homework studies show only a **correlation** between homework and academic success. He points out that this doesn't prove that homework *causes* academic success. Successful pupils tend to be in more advanced classes where more homework is given. Pupils may also do more homework *because* they do better at school, rather than the other way round.

Other studies, including an international study done by David Baker and Gerald LeTendre, found that frequency and amount of homework was negatively correlated with academic success. This means that doing more homework was associated with lower test results, rather than higher ones. In the words of the authors, "More homework may actually undermine national achievement."

The claim: Homework has benefits beyond school performance

The reasoning

Even if homework doesn't help pupils do better at school, it can help them develop other skills, such as learning on their own and organizing and managing their time. These skills are useful for life at and beyond school. Think about your own experience. If a teacher asks you to write an essay or read a book, you have to plan how you will do that task in the given time. Your plan may have many steps that will take days or even weeks. Planning projects and carrying them out requires self-discipline and organizational ability. Advocates for homework say that it's important to give it so that pupils will have to develop these skills on their own, out of school.

> *Homework and time management*

When pupils have to juggle multiple tasks, such as homework and after-school activities, they need to develop the ability to make and follow schedules—an essential skill for adulthood.

The evidence

Few studies support the claim that homework helps to develop non-academic skills. One study, done in 1965, showed that pupils who did more homework had better study and time management skills than those who studied in class. Otherwise, there's not a lot of research to support this claim. However, you may be able to come up with examples from your own or your friends' experience to back up this argument. Can you think of a time when doing a piece of homework taught you something about managing your time and planning a project?

On the other hand...

It may be that homework actually keeps children from learning to manage their time. With their after-school hours planned out for them, and homework only adding to that burden, many children have little or no free time to pursue their own interests, read books that really interest them, or just relax.

The claim: Homework keeps parents involved with children's schooling

The reasoning

Because homework is something that children do at home, often with help or supervision from their parents, homework is an important bridge that connects home and school. A lot of good research shows that children perform better at school when parents are supportive of and involved in their education.

The evidence

Homework does involve parents in their children's education. Schools often ask parents to monitor their children's progress in doing their homework. When parents supervise homework, they know exactly what their children are learning in class and can answer questions and engage children in discussions about those topics. If parents can reinforce school lessons in other ways at home, it increases the chances that children will remember the information they learn at school.

On the other hand...

Homework's not the only way to involve parents in school. Phone calls, letters home, and parent-teacher meetings are some other, possibly better, ways to involve parents. Also, parents are often tempted to do the homework for their children. This does not result in the children learning anything except how to persuade their parents to do homework for them.

Understanding the research

You've read a lot so far in this book about different studies relating to homework. But how do these researchers get to their conclusions, and what kind of methods do they use? Most studies about homework use what's called an **experimental design**. Perhaps you've done experiments in a science class. Experiments in educational research are similar in some ways, and different in others. In educational research, you conduct an experiment by comparing a group of pupils who meet a certain condition with another group of pupils who do not meet that condition. For example, you might find a group of pupils who have been assigned to read a particular book and compare them to another group who have not read it. The group that has not read the book is known as the **control group**.

Researchers collect information, or **data**, using **surveys** and questionnaires about the participants in their studies. Then they look at all the data, comparing the experimental group to the control group. This shows what effects, if any, the experiment had. Many researchers who study homework's effects give homework to the experimental group and not to the control group. Then they set an exam or just look at the students' marks to see how the homework group did compared to the non-homework group.

Conduct your own experiment

As you've already read, there is substantial disagreement about how much homework pupils do. You can do some research of your own to find answers to this and other topics. You can find this out by doing a survey of your friends and classmates. The first step is to design a survey. Think of a few questions you'd like to ask, and print them on a piece of paper. Consider using a **scale**, where people who respond to your survey choose from a set of responses. For example, you might use a question like this:

Questionnaire

	30 mins or less	***30 mins–1 hour***	***1–2 hours***	***More than 2 hours***
How much homework do you do every night?				

Once you've surveyed some classmates, you can calculate the results by converting your findings to percentages. Let's say you surveyed ten classmates. Of those ten, five said they did 1–2 hours of homework. That means that $5/10$, or $1/2$, or 50 percent of your classmates did 1–2 hours of homework.

There's no reason to stop there. You could add more questions to your survey to gather more information. For example, you could ask friends and classmates if they feel that homework is not helpful, slightly helpful, or very helpful for improving academic achievement, study skills, or any other concept you'd like to measure.

> *Collecting information*

Come to your own conclusions about how much homework pupils do by conducting your own survey. Get the opinions of other pupils, teachers, and parents.

> *How important is homework for success?*

Graduation day is always a proud moment, when students reflect on all the work that they did to earn their degrees or diplomas. But is all that work, including all the homework, really worth it?

Homework Pros And Cons

Children are very busy these days. They have jobs, take care of their younger brothers or sisters, play musical instruments, attend classes in dance or art, or play sport. Sometimes they may just want to relax in front of the television or with a good book. If you're at school, there are a lot of demands on your time. You may have a piece of homework on the same night as a concert. Or you may just be tired and in need of sleep on the night your teacher asks you to read a story. How do you decide what is the best use of your time and why? What if you decide not to do your homework?

In this chapter, we'll explore the effects of the choices children make about how to spend their time. We'll also look at what's at stake, by examining the costs and benefits of graduating from secondary school and university or college. To have an informed opinion about homework, it's important to know about the pros and cons of doing (or not doing) it.

How much is too much?

Many parents want schools to set a lot of homework. They are concerned that unless their children work hard they won't be able to compete with others to get into university and find good jobs. As countries move towards standards-based education, there is a lot of pressure on teachers to cover all the curriculum. This can make them set more homework, just to fit everything in.

But there is also pressure to reduce the homework load. Parents of children in primary school are increasingly concerned about the amount of homework their children are given. They worry that excessive homework will cause stress and make their children lose interest in school. Professor Harris Cooper of Duke University has expressed concern that too much homework can overload family and outside actitivies: "Homework can be stressful because it's something that families have to fit into their lifestyles. For some families, it's difficult to figure out how to carve out the time that children need to do it."

> *Benefits of other activities?*

Young people are involved in so much more than academic school work. Activities such as sport are important for improving physical wellbeing and for building skills such as teamwork.

> *Does homework interfere with sleep?*

Adolescents still need a lot of sleep. However, there are only a fixed number of hours in the day. Pupils who don't get a proper night's sleep don't do as well at school.

Lost opportunities

The problem of balancing homework with other activities is a very real one. Depending who you ask, the average 11–15 year-old child does between 20 minutes and 3 hours of homework every night. That time could be spent on other activities—activities that are good for improving health (such as sport), good for balance and concentration (such as dance), and good for learning and expressing creativity (such as art). The trouble may be that children are increasingly spending time on activities with little or no physical or educational value, such as watching TV. The average child watches 2 hours of TV every night, and there's little doubt that this time could be better spent. At the same time, it's important to have time to relax and unwind. It's not healthy to move from activity to activity so much that you feel stressed all the time.

How do you manage your time?

Without knowing it, you're an expert in time management. Every day, you make choices about how to spend your day. Let's say you get out of school at 3.30, and have to go to bed at 10.00. That leaves you with six and a half hours, or less if your bedtime is earlier. How would you organize that time for the following activities?

- Homework (0–2 hours)
- Dinner (1 hour)
- Athletic practice or after-school club (1 hour)
- Watching television (0–2 hours)
- Talking on the phone (0–2 hours)
- Helping with chores (0–2 hours)
- Reading for pleasure (0–2 hours)

What's the most important item on this list? Why? What's the least important? Why? Are there times when certain activities are more important than others—for example, if you need to practise for a forthcoming concert or look after a younger sibling?

Try keeping a diary of how you spend your time after school. What activities do you do? How would you like to change your time allocation? What activities would you like to add or drop? What activities would you like to spend more or less time on? How would you achieve that?

What's the value of success?

Debates about the importance and amount of homework aren't just about succeeding or failing in the classroom. The bigger issue is how well pupils will perform in exams. Countries want their children to succeed at school. Governments and communities have an obligation to try to help the next generation. Also, educated populations generally help their communities and countries by generating wealth, making scientific and cultural advances, and bringing other benefits.

But is it fair or realistic to tie a nation's economic prospects to children's ability to do their homework? Is this really what school is for? Some people say that good schools help the economy remain strong and keep the good jobs in the country. Similar arguments were made after the Sputnik launch in 1957 and in the 1983 report, *A Nation at Risk*. The idea is that nations need to preserve their **economic competitiveness**. This term describes a country's ability to compete with other nations in creating jobs and selling lots of goods.

> *Choosing a career*

Getting a good education affects your options for the future. Usually, the more educated you are, the more choices you have later in life for careers. In 2005 the British government's Labour Force Survey found that the average university graduate earns about £7,000 more per year than a non-graduate.

But there is not necessarily a relationship between a nation's educational achievement and the health of its economy. In fact one researcher, Gerald Bracey, showed that there was no correlation between pupils' results in maths and science and a nation's overall economic competitiveness. But others argue that it's common sense that a nation with bad results in maths and science cannot do as well at making and marketing new inventions.

There's no denying the fact educational success can dramatically affect how much money you earn later in life. Pupils who finish secondary school earn 30 percent more than their peers who drop out. That pay gap increases substantially for university graduates, who earn significantly more than people without a degree. This helps to explain some of people's concern about homework.

> *Making discoveries*

Many people think it's important for countries to have an educated population so they can make advances in science and technology. These advances might save lives, boost the economy, or help the environment.

> *Succeeding in different fields*

Not all secondary school work is designed to send pupils to university. Schools also teach vocational skills. These students are learning about surveying in the construction industry.

Stress is bad for you

Stressed out about homework? It could be bad for your health. Stress can affect your ability to sleep and properly digest food. It can also give you headaches, chest pains, and muscle tension. Stress may cause you to cry, be angry with friends or family, be confused, have poor judgement, or have difficulty remembering things.

But homework doesn't have to cause stress. You will sometimes feel worried or stressed when you face difficult situations. But identifying the causes of your stress, and working to manage and reduce them, can change your feelings of stress into feelings of achievement and accomplishment. Spending time relaxing or even meditating will also help you reduce the feelings and symptoms associated with stress.

Is it worth it?

Should schools and pupils be responsible for the economic health of a country? If doing a little extra homework every night might increase the chances that someone will do well at school, and perhaps go to college or university, wouldn't it be worth it?

> *Is homework worthwhile?*

Work outside school doesn't have to be boring and painful. It can be enjoyable and informative, as shown by this group of pupils working on a project together. Does homework have a bad reputation, or is it just plain bad?

What Do You Think?

After reading about homework, it's time to put the information together to draw your own conclusions. In this chapter, we'll try to help you form your opinion about homework by looking closely at a few different examples and summarizing the main points from the text. You'll also learn ways to have your own debate with friends or classmates about the pros and cons of homework.

The central question of this book has been: Is homework a waste of time? After all this, you should be able to develop your own informed answer to that question. As part of that, you'll need to question what you think about homework. As we noted at the beginning of this book, you probably do a fair amount of homework and have your own opinions about it. But part of becoming a critical thinker means questioning everything, including your own pre-existing opinions.

You'll also need to review and consider the evidence. This may mean doing some more research on your own. To help you with that process, we've included a section called "Find Out More". This section lists books, websites, and even a film that may help you get more information about the benefits and drawbacks of homework.

> *Teaching to the exam?*

Homework can be a good way to give pupils extra practice for exams. The problem is that most exams just measure knowledge of what's in the exam. They don't always measure other skills, such as problem solving, critical thinking, creativity, and artistic ability. If teachers concentrate only on preparing pupils for exams, they may fail to help them learn other important skills.

How does homework score?

Not all homework is the same. There's a big difference between doing one worksheet and reading a novel. Whether homework is a waste of time or not can depend on what kind of homework we're talking about. The table on the next page briefly compares four basic kinds of homework. You can also assess the pros and cons of other kinds of homework. Are some kinds of homework better than others? Or is it all pretty much the same?

What about testing?

In the chapter "History of Homework", you learned about the trend towards standards-based education. As countries set higher standards for education, they also tend to require students to take more exams. These are said to create **accountability** for schools. This means using testing to see if schools are meeting standards. Exams can be an important and useful way to assess how well pupils, teachers, and schools are doing. Much of the research that supports homework's academic benefits measures how well pupils do in exams after they've done homework on the tested material. They tend to do better, which makes sense. If you're going to be tested on multiplication, memorizing multiplication tables will help you score well. But some people say that "teaching to the exam" can lead to more boring lessons, and the pressure to improve exam results may encourage teachers to set more homework.

Judging the work

Type of homework	*Pros*	*Cons*
Doing a worksheet	- Repeats and reinforces concepts from class or the textbook. - Can be completed quickly and easily by students. - Convenient for teachers to hand out and mark.	- Often assigned as "busy work" for students without clear goals from teachers. - Doesn't help with deep thought or understanding; mostly designed for memorizing. - Usually boring.
Making a poster	- Students use different kinds of skill, including art and design skills. - Teaches summarization for including text on posters. - Good project for group work, so pupils learn to work with others.	- Often requires buying new materials or equipment. - May not produce new insights about the material; just a chance to give surface details. - Difficult to organize with other students to do group work outside school.
Writing an essay	- Helps students develop essential writing skills. - May teach research skills for gathering information to support a topic. - Teaches organizational skills and how to focus deeply on an issue.	- A long project without much supervision. - Pupils may not have access to the resources they need (library, Internet). - May be too difficult and overwhelming for many students.
Independent reading	- Depending on the book, can be interesting and informative for pupils. - Encourages pupils to learn to read on their own. - If pupils choose their own books, they're likely to enjoy reading more.	- Depending on the book, can be boring. - Difficult for teachers to evaluate and assess if pupils read and what they learn. - Books pupils choose on their own may not be challenging enough.

Why do teachers set homework?

When teachers set homework, many pupils complain. But most teachers set homework because they think it's important. Also, it may be school policy that they must set it. Retired teacher Lisa Morehouse explains why she used to give homework in an article published in the magazine *Edutopia*: "In the twelve years I taught in low-income urban and rural schools," she writes, "I saw my students extend their skills, their understanding of their communities, and their sense of themselves when given well-crafted take-home assignments." Most teachers work hard to set homework that will be interesting, useful, and meaningful.

> *Good teacher or boring teacher?*

Good teachers help pupils engage with the learning process.

What do good teachers do?

Most children can identify teachers that they think are particularly good. And every child can name a teacher they think is a bad teacher. Sometimes homework has a lot to do with these ratings. But pupils rarely stop to consider the value of homework from the perspective of the teacher. Remember that critical thinkers must try to see issues from multiple points of view, including the those of other people.

Next time you get homework you don't like, stop for a moment and put yourself in your teacher's shoes. If you were the teacher, what would you be trying to accomplish with the homework? Then consider whether the homework is effective in reaching those goals.

Putting it all together

This book presents many perspectives on homework to help you develop informed opinions about the issue. We've learned that homework wasn't always an important part of education, that there is evidence for and against the benefits of homework, and that homework may take time from other pursuits. We've considered the importance of success at school and university for personal and national gain.

But we haven't answered our main question: Is homework a waste of time? That's for you to decide. Answering these questions will help you to sort out your ideas about homework. As you think about each question, try to add reasoning and evidence to your answers.

- Does homework help academic performance?
- Are pupils doing more homework these days than ever before?
- Do pupils start doing homework younger than in the past?
- Does homework teach non-academic skills such as self-discipline?
- Does homework involve parents in their children's education? In a good way or a bad way?
- How much homework is too much?
- Are there good kinds of homework and bad kinds of homework? If so, what are they?

If you think that homework is a waste of time, consider how else we should spend that time. For example, what if eliminating homework would result in children watching more television? On the other hand, if you think homework is a good use of time, consider the activities it takes time away from. What if eliminating homework encouraged pupils to read and learn on their own? Is it better to do work that's set, or to come up with your own projects?

How to debate

There are three important parts of a debate in any format. First, all participants must be able to make arguments to defend their views. Arguments should have three parts: an assertion, reasoning, and evidence. Second, participants should make sure that they respond to opposing arguments. It's not enough just to make an argument for your side; you also have to answer what the other side says. This is called **refutation**. Third, it is important to take notes during any debate or discussion. This will allow you to track arguments as they're made and prepare to respond to the other side.

> *Talk it out!*

Now that you've researched, read, and thought about the pros and cons of homework, consider organizing a debate or discussion in class or with friends to further refine your ideas and test your opinions against others.

There are many different ways to have a debate or discussion. A few different formats are given here. Each has a particular set of rules. You can change the rules for the number of participants or the amount of time you have available for an event.

Two-sided debate

One side—the ***proposition*** or affirmative—makes a case. This team must prove that the topic is more likely to be true. The opposition or negative side argues against the case. Each participant makes a speech, with the teams taking turns.

The proposition team speaks first and last. The opening proposition speaker states a case, and the first opposition speaker refutes it. Second speakers continue with their team's points and refute new points from the other side. The final speeches summarize each team's best arguments in favour of its case and against the other side. With six students, you might follow this format:

First speaker, proposition – 5 minutes

First speaker, opposition – 5 minutes

Second speaker, proposition – 5 minutes

Second speaker, opposition – 5 minutes

Third speaker, opposition – 3 minutes

Third speaker, proposition – 3 minutes

It is possible to add question and comment time by the opposing side or a class or audience during, in between, or after the speeches.

Discussion

A panel discussion is designed to inform an audience. A group, or panel, of pupils presents and challenges ideas about an issue. Pupils speak for themselves and may agree or disagree with the opinions of other panel members. There is an overall time limit, perhaps 30 minutes, for the discussion. A moderator can ask questions and keep the discussion moving. Audience questions may be added afterwards.

Open forum

This format is effective for a class or large group. A moderator leads an open discussion on a range of topics. Members of the audience may present new ideas, add to what others have presented, or refute any issue. This format quickly introduces a variety of ideas.

An individual or group may judge a debate, voting on the outcome. For larger discussions, you may ask an audience which person did the best job and why.

Try out your opinion

Now that you've got a solid, well-supported opinion about homework, try it out on a few people. If you think homework is a waste of time, try convincing your teacher or your parents. See if you can answer their arguments convincingly. If you think homework is a good thing, try convincing a friend who hates homework. Try to have solid responses to his or her objections. Once you've tried this process, you're ready to have a more formal debate. In fact, you've already started!

Find Out More

Books

- *The End of Homework*. Etta Kralovec and John Buell (Beacon Press, 2001)
- *Homework: The Evidence*, Sausan Hallam (Institute of Education, 2004)
- *The Homework Myth*, Alfie Kohn (Da Capo Lifelong, 2006)

Websites

- *Official Guidelines*

  http://www.parentscentre.gov.uk/educationandlearning/whatchildrenlearn/learningathomeoutsideschool/homework/

  This official government site gives guidelines for the amount of homework pupils of all ages should be doing.
- *National Foundation for Educational Research*
  http://www.ufer.ac.uk/reserch-areas/pims-data/summaries/hwk-review-of-studies-on-homework.cfm
  This review on the website of the National Foundation for Educational Research was commissioned by Ofsted. It set out to identify the best evidence from recent research into homework.
- *Alfie Kohn's Home Page*
  http://www.alfiekohn.org
  Author Alfie Kohn has written many articles about the problems associated with homework.
- *Home Invasion*
  http://www.theage.com.au/news/National/Home-invasion/2005/02/04/1107476790672.html
  This article, from the Australian newspaper *The Age*, is a good summary of both sides of the homework debate.
- *Pupils' Perspectives on Homework*
  http://education.guardian.co.uk/schools/story/0,,1144127,00.html
  This page from the *Guardian* has information for and against homework. It is a reprint of a chapter from a book called *Homework: The Evidence*.
- *April Foolishness: The 20th Anniversary of A Nation At Risk*

- *April Foolishness: The 20th Anniversary of A Nation At Risk*
  http://www.pdkintl.org/kappan/k0304bra.htm
  This article, by author Gerald Bracey, discusses education, homework, and educational competitiveness.

Film

- *Stand And Deliver* (1988)

Glossary

accountability	idea that individuals and organizations (like schools) are responsible for their actions and may have to explain their actions and policies to others
argument	series of statements supporting one side of an issue or topic. Contains an assertion, reasoning, and evidence.
assumption	claim or statement about an issue
bias	preference or tendency. Being biased usually means that a source leans towards one side more than another.
causality	relationship that shows causes and their effects
control group	in research, a group of people that is used as a basis of comparison. They are compared to another group that receives a treatment or has to perform a task.
correlation	link between two elements that correspond, or happen together. For example, "Good grades are often correlated with serious studying." It can imply a causal relationship, but not necessarily.
cortical map	network of pathways between cells in your brain. The brain creates these pathways depending on how you use your brain.
counterintuitive	contrary to common sense or usual beliefs
critical thinking	process that involves careful consideration of many perspectives on an issue
data	collection of facts
economic competitiveness	country's ability to compete with other countries in creating jobs and selling lots of goods
evidence	material that supports the reasoning for an argument. It can include examples, statistics, expert testimony, and personal stories.

experimental design specific way of doing research, in which people are assigned randomly to participate in a *control group* or a *treatment group*.

mediocrity description of things of an average or bad quality

proposition something put forward as true for discussion or debate

reasoning part of an argument that supports one's point or opinion by answering the question "because"

refutation answer back given in an argument or debate

scale measuring device with a series of different ratings. On surveys, researchers use scales with different categories such as Never, Sometimes, and Often.

standards-based education holding teachers and students to standards that are made and enforced by governments

statistics science of collecting, organizing, and interpreting data. It can also refer to numbers used to express different things, especially in percentages.

survey tool for gathering information by asking questions

time on task amount of time spent on a particular activity

Index